Battle Ready

Preparation to Purpose

Sandra Carrizales

Forward by Yolanda Myers

Published by Sandra Carrizales

Battle Ready

CONTENTS

Prayer

Father God, I turn to you as the solid rock on which I
stand
I asked you to lead me in the way in which I should
I seek your guidance and revelation
I look to you for wisdom and correction
I don't want to take a step without knowing you are
leading me
The decisions I need to make must be the right ones
Father keep me from making mistakes
Even when I must make a quick decision, help me to do
so with
Great accuracy
Thank you, Lord, for the wisdom and knowledge you so
gracefully give
Make me sensitive to the leading of the Holy Spirit

Blessed be the Lord my strength which teacheth my hands to war, and my fingers to fight: My goodness, and my fortress; My high tower, and my deliverer; My shield, and he in whom I trust; Who subdueth my people under me.

I am so happy and excited to introduce this extraordinary work, a labor of love, faith, and unwavering devotion, written by my dear friend of 40 years, Sandra Carrizales. As I reflect on our journey together, I am humble. I have had the opportunity to see her remarkable transformation into the woman of unshakeable faith, a true powerhouse in her own right, and a vessel through which the manifestation of God's presence shines radiantly.

In this book, you will embark on a profound journey guided by Sandra's spiritual conviction and self-reflection. Her ability to articulate the intertwined relationship of the divine and the human experience is nothing short of awe-inspiring. As she unravels the complexity of the manifestations of God, she invites us to explore the very essence of our purpose, urging us to recognize the divine being within us all.

Through the years, I have had the privilege of witnessing the countless hours Sandra dedicated to studying, praying, and seeking a deeper understanding of the Word of God. Her passion for spiritual growth has been a beacon of inspiration, reminding us of all of the boundless power of faith. As Sisters in Christ, we have shared our joys, our sorrows, and our spiritual journeys. In this book, Sandra encourages transparency to all who seek to understand the intricate tapestry of

God's manifestation in our lives. Her words give a glimpse of the deep connection that unites us all as the children of our Heavenly Father.

As you read these pages of Sandra's book, I encourage you to open your heart and mind to the wisdom she imparts. You will find in this book, a profound testament to the transformative power of faith and a reminder that the manifestation of God is not distant, but ever-present in our lives.

May Sandra's journey inspire you as it has inspired me, and may her words lead you to a deeper understanding of God's goodness and his divine appointments for us all.

With love and faith,
Yoli Myers

Battle Ready is written out of obedience to the Lord. A year and half before this book was written, the Lord told me to write everything He said. He said, "One day you will need evidence."

February 9, 2022, was the day I bowed low before the Lord and fully surrendered. From that day forward He has instructed me to speak His word. This book is a collection of stories that were written by the hand of the Lord. Divine connections, spiritual warfare, loss, deliverance, restoration, and redemption.

July 14, 2023, I heard the Lord say, write the book. The title will be Battle Ready. The day I sat down to draft this book, the Lord said it is already written. The evidence, the words written in my journals, the situations orchestrated by the Lord, and my testimonies, serve as the context for this book.

There is a message in the following pages for his people. My prayer is that the stories in the pages to follow will encourage you to trust in the Lord, to have faith in the Lord and to believe.

God is no respecter of persons. If He can bring me through to the other side, He can do the same for you.

Romans 2:11
For there is no respect of persons with God.

Introduction

We all have a story to tell about our life. For some of us, God has rewritten our stories. These are stories of obedience, sacrifice, redemption, restoration, deliverance, restitution and so much more.

Revelation 12:11
And they overcame him by the blood of the Lamb, and by the word
Of their testimony, and they loved not their lives unto the death

Twelve years!! This is the amount of time it took for me to become Battle Ready. It was not only a process, but preparation. In those twelve years, I never imagined I would be where I am today. It was a process of discovery and deliverance. Discovering the Father, the Son, and the Holy Spirit. Discovering who God has called me to be. A process of deliverance from the things that kept me bound for so long. Also, a process of renewing my mind. If I had to do it again, I would not change a thing.

The old me has passed away. Despite all the bad choices we make, God gives us a new name. He changed me from the inside out. So that I would never be the same again. He calls us, daughter, worthy, victorious, forgiven, loved, redeemed, restored, healed, and more than a conqueror.

During this process, the Lord taught me as He was writing the testimonies of my life, that He had someone else in mind. He said this journey was so much bigger than me. If these stories written on these pages only help one person, I have completed the instructions and assignment the Lord has given me.

I am here to encourage you to tell your story. Even if parts of it are not pretty or neatly packaged, people need to hear it.

1

The Reintroduction

Allow me to reintroduce myself.

July 29, 2011, I left my home, my family, my niece whom I loved dearly, my friends and my past. We moved from Texas to South Dakota to be with my daughter's father.

Prior to becoming a mother, Sandra was the party girl. Always traveling, hanging out with friends, clubbing, drinking, having the time of her life. Life was good. I had no responsibilities other than to myself. I had nobody to answer to. I lived alone and I did what I wanted to do.

But that life came to a screeching halt. When I became pregnant with my daughter. When she was born, I became Olivia's mom. I had lost my identity in becoming a mother. I had a daughter at thirty-eight years old. Before I had my daughter, I thought I knew who Sandra was. I didn't. It was a major adjustment. After the birth of my daughter, I was diagnosed with Postpartum depression. I thought this was normal after giving birth to a child. I now realize for me it was an attack from the enemy. An attack on my identity.

My doctor recommended that I see a therapist. Thankfully, the therapist was a woman of God. By the grace of God, He used her therapy sessions to help me see that I could be more than a mom.

When I moved to South Dakota the journey to find my identity began. One day I read a quote that said, "One day you will tell your story of how you've overcome what you are going through now, and it will become part of someone else's survival guide."

One day the Lord spoke to me and said, sharing your stories gives me glory.

Matthew 19:29
And everyone who has left houses or siblings or father or mother or children or farms for My name's sake, will receive many times as much and will inherit eternal life.

This book is my testimony. How God brought me through to the other side, the season where the oil was produced. The season, where the Lord exposed the enemy, taught me to war in the Spirit and prepared me for battle through His word.

Our ministry is found where we have been broken, and our testimony is found where we have been restored.

Psalms 144:1-2 NIV
Praise be to the Lord my Rock, who trains my hands for war, my fingers for battle. He is my loving God and my fortress, my stronghold and my deliverer, my shield, in whom I take refuge, who subdues peoples under me.

As a child, I was raised by my grandmother. Three things I learned from my grandmother were to believe in God, family is important and to be generous.

Growing up I knew about God. I attended church camp in the summers when I was a teenager. I made the decision to be baptized at an early age. I would pray but only on occasion. It had been many years since I had been in a church. I only went to church for weddings or funerals. I knew about God, but I clearly was not walking with him. I would only pray to God when I needed something.

Here I was, a former party girl who did not want children. Truth be told, I thought I could not have children. I was ok with being an Auntie. It appeared as though I was living the "good life." I went where I wanted when I wanted. I was fine with being single with no responsibility other than for myself.

My life has been very untraditional. Growing up I was raised by my grandmother. My grandmother raised me as her own. As an adult, my grandmother would constantly tell me, "Even if you never get married, have a child." That was her prayer. That I would someday have a child. People might say, why would her grandmother say that to her own grandchild?? Or think it strange that a grandmother would want her grand-daughter to have a child out of wedlock. Well, her explanation was, she did not want me to grow old alone. She wanted me to have someone who would look after me as I got older.

My grandmother must have had a good thing going on with God. Her prayer was answered. God blessed me with a beautiful, healthy daughter. She has been the greatest joy and blessing of my life. I am so grateful my grandmother lived to see and know my daughter. It was a blessing to see the love between my grandmother and daughter. Although things in my life did not happen in the traditional sense, that was the path I had to take to get to where I am today.

There are times in my life when I am overwhelmed by the goodness of God. How He left the ninety-nine to rescue me. A former party girl, lost in the world, who did not want children, and had no responsibility other than to herself.

Matthew 18:12

"What do you think? If a man owns a hundred sheep, and one of them

Wanders away, will he not leave the ninety-nine on the hills and go to

Look for the one that wandered off?

I thought I was living my best life. I used to say, "those were the good ol' days." Really?? What was so "good" about them? I was so lost in the world. My life was a mess. I never imagined God would use me in the way He has. How God has used me to help others. At times, I felt so unworthy of His grace and mercy. Then He reminded me of the woman at the well.

John 4:7 - 42

When a Samaritan woman came to draw water, Jesus said to her, "Will you give me a drink?" The Samaritan woman said to him, "You are a Jew, and I am a Samaritan woman. How can you ask me for a drink?" Jesus answered her, "If you knew the gift of God and who it is that asks you for a drink, you would have asked him, and he would have given you living water." "Sir," the woman said, "you have nothing to draw with and the well is deep. Where can you get this living water? Are you greater than our father Jacob, who gave us the well and drank from it himself, as did also his sons and his livestock?" Jesus answered, "Everyone who drinks this water will be thirsty again, but whoever drinks the water I give them will never thirst. Indeed, the water I give them will become in them a spring of water welling up to eternal life." The woman said to him, "Sir, give me this water so that I won't get thirsty and have to keep coming here to draw water." He told her, "Go, call your husband and come back." "I have no husband," she replied. Jesus said to her, "You are right when you say you have no husband. The fact is, you have had five husbands, and the man you now have is not your husband. What you have just said is quite true." "Sir," the woman said, "I can see that you are a prophet. Our ancestors worshiped on this mountain, but you Jews claim that the place where we must worship is in Jerusalem." "Woman," Jesus replied, "believe me, a time is coming when you will worship the Father neither on this mountain nor in Jerusalem. You Samaritans worship what you do not know; we worship what we do know, for salvation is from the Jews.

Yet a time is coming and has now come when the true worshipers will worship the Father in the Spirit and in truth, for they are the kind of worshipers the Father seeks. God is spirit, and his worshipers must worship in the Spirit and in truth." The woman said, "I know that Messiah" (called Christ) "is coming. When he comes, he will explain everything to us." Then Jesus declared, "I, the one speaking to you—I am he."

Then, leaving her water jar, the woman went back to the town and said to the people, "Come, see a man who told me everything I ever did. Could this be the Messiah?" They came out of the town and made their way toward him. Many of the Samaritans from that town believed in him because of the woman's testimony, "He told me everything I ever did." So, when the Samaritans came to him, they urged him to stay with them, and he stayed two days. And because of his words many more became believers. They said to the woman, "We no longer believe just because of what you said; now we have heard for ourselves, and we know that this man really is the Savior of the world."

To get to where I am today, I had to ask Jesus to give me this water so that I would never be thirsty again. I had to reach for the hem of his garment, I had to sit at the feet of Jesus, I had to surrender to him, I had to die to my flesh, so that God could be God. I had to pursue and endure.

For so many years, I was stuck, bound. I delayed the blessings God has for me. But the more I got to know him, the more I spent time with him. He began to change who I was, into who He wanted me to be. The change began from the inside out. Despite all my bad choices, my impatience and sometimes my unbelief, God showed me mercy and grace.

This walk with God has been an incredible journey.

2

Turning point

I want to start by asking this question. Have you ever found it difficult to pray for yourself? Think about that for a second.

In 2019, the Lord sat me down and told me to move in silence. What did that mean? Why did the Lord want me to move in silence? Well, truth be told, I was asking everyone to pray for me, but I never prayed for myself. I did not know how to pray for myself. I would pray for others and see those prayers answered. So, I knew God heard my prayers. Why were my prayers not being answered? I was asking people to pray for me. Were they not praying for me like I prayed for them?

This is what I thought about prayer. I thought praying for myself was selfish. I thought it had to be formal. I learned that it doesn't. God just wants us to have a conversation with him. The way you speak to a friend. Some days, it is "Lord, what do you want me to know today? Or, Lord, what do you have for me today? I talk to him every day. Even if it's a short conversation.

The day God told me to move in silence, He also told me, don't tell everyone your business. Tell ME!

Jeremiah 33:3

Call to Me, and I will answer you, and show you great and mighty things, which you do not know

This is what I learned in the process:

1. Some things should simply exist between me and God. No one else, until the Lord releases me to share.
2. Normalize not making announcements about everything I am going through, doing, or planning to do.
3. To become spiritually mature, I had to be quiet so I could hear from the Lord.
4. I shouldn't ask everyone to pray for me because not everyone IS anointed to pray for me.

John 14:13-14

And whatsoever ye shall ask in My name, that will I do, that the Father may be glorified in the son. If ye shall ask anything in My name I will do it.

This was the turning point for me. This is where I began to really understand what it meant to sit at the feet of Jesus. He wanted me to speak to him so He could speak to me.

He wanted me to spend more time with him. Since then, I have seen the manifestation of many prayers. This is where I began to build a relationship with the Father, the Son, and the Holy Spirit.

Matthew 7:7-8

Ask, and it shall be given you, see, and ye shall find; knock, and it shall be opened unto you
For everyone that asketh, receiveth; and he that seeketh findeth and to him that knocketh it shall be opened.

This is where I began to hear from God. This is where I began to experience revelation. This is where I began to heal. Where I began to experience the deeper things of God. I don't want to give too much attention to the enemy, but I will say he had me believing praying for myself was selfish. Why?? He didn't want me to get to a place where I would learn to pray for myself. The enemy knew the power and authority I would have over his plots and schemes. But by the Spirit of God, I can now pray fervently over myself. I have taken power away from the enemy.

Yet, there was still more to learn about prayer. The Lord has blessed me with a covering through my Pastor and mentor. He has also divinely connected me to four powerful women of God who stand in agreement with me. One thing that disturbs my spirit is when I see people post or hear them say something like 'please pray God knows the need' or 'unspoken prayer requests.'

For a moment, when I would pray, I would say something like, Lord you know the amount I need. You know what I need. One day I reached out to my sisters in Christ, I said please stand in agreement with me for the funding I need for this particular project. I said to them God knows the number, He knows the amount.

The Lord spoke to me and said, you're being too passive with your prayers. He said you're doing the very thing you say you don't like to see or hear people do.

The Lord convicted me and corrected me. I had to confess this to my sisters in Christ who are my covering. This is the power of correction, confession, and obedience. The original amount I was told I needed for the project was ten thousand to fifteen thousand. After I shared the amount I needed for the project, the Lord began to move on my behalf. As the days went by, the amount began to decrease. When it was all said and done, I only needed a few hundred dollars to start the project. I saw the literal hand of God move on my behalf.

What should have taken six months to a year only took sixty-nine days. The favor of God was on this project. It was a vision He had given me. At the appointed time, God made it happen. At this moment, He reminded me that I am a daughter of the King. He is my Father. I can go to him for anything, big or small. Believe that God is going to do it. But know that it's already done. God wanted me to make my requests known to Him, no one else. He wanted me, as His daughter, to ask Him specifically for what I needed.

Philippians 4:6
Be careful for nothing, but in everything by prayer and supplication with thanksgiving, let your requests Be made known unto God. And the peace of God, which passeth all understanding shall
Keep your hearts and minds through Christ Jesus

3

The Infirmity

I had someone reach out to me by text. In that text, it said "pray for me." They had recently been to the doctor and mentioned what the doctor had discovered. I will pray for anyone who asks. So, I asked, what is going on? They told me about all of the physical things they were dealing with. Then I asked, how do you feel about what the doctor said? Their response was, I have faith and I have been praying.

My next question was, what are you doing to take part in your own healing? They said they were praying. As we continued our conversation they made the comment, "I'm just waiting on the Lord." My response to that comment was, "did you ever think maybe the Lord is waiting on you?

There was a reason God wanted me to ask the question, what they were doing to take part in your own healing. That question took me back to the time I had to take part in my own healing. Not just my own healing but my own deliverance. What I thought was an isolated incident, was just the beginning.

Unbeknownst to me, the enemy had launched a full-on attack on my body. It literally happened without warning. I was fine all day, then at night it happened suddenly.

December 20, 2020, I began to have excruciating back pain. I have a high tolerance for pain. But this was unlike anything I had ever experienced. I could not walk, sit, stand, or sleep. All I could do was cry. It can only be described as labor pains. Even though I did not go through labor with my daughter, this is what I imagined the pain would be without an epidural.

At the time, I was working a full-time job at a bank. Since the time my daughter was two years old, I have been blessed with the opportunity to be a stay-at-home mom. Over the years, I worked part time in hospitality. During this season of my life, I needed something more. I thought, since my daughter was in middle school, it was time for me to work full time. How can I say I am a stay-at-home mom with my daughter in middle school? Those were my thoughts and that was my plan; to go back to work full time.

The next day, I called in to work, called my Chiropractor hoping I could get some relief. The day after that I returned to work.

January 10, 2021, I had another episode. Same as the first time. Coincidentally, it was a Sunday night as well. Just like the first time. This time the pain lasted longer than one day. I was out of work for an entire week.

January 29, 2021, I called in to work, still experiencing back pain. At this point, I decided to see my doctor. She ordered X-Rays to ensure there was nothing else. The doctor then recommended physical therapy. I finally return to work on February 8, 2021. Over the next two weeks, I am going to physical therapy, Chiropractor and working full time.

During this time, my doctor requested an MRI. However, the MRI was denied by my insurance. I returned to the doctor's office on February 19, 2021. I had enough. I wanted some relief from the constant pain. I told her I had to take a leave of absence from work until we were able to find the cause. After I went on leave, I was approved for an MRI. I was also referred to the Spine Center.

The night of February 24, 2021, in our mentorship group, we went through the process of anointing our homes. We had anointed our homes before, but this night was different. My prayer was "Lord, if there is anything that is not of you, eradicate it." That night, the issue of laziness was revealed. I did not understand what that meant. How could I have an issue with laziness? I was working a full-time job.

At the time, I took part in a book club. In this book we were reading about strongholds. When I reviewed my notes from the book club, I had written in my journal, "What are my strongholds and what's holding me back?" I remember saying to myself, "I don't have any strongholds." Not realizing at the time when we anointed our homes, the Lord had revealed to me the issue of laziness. I was clueless. But that is what pleased the enemy. I was clueless, I could not move in the purpose and plans God had for my life.

After multiple doctor's appointments, chiropractor appointments, physical therapy, x rays, and an MRI, all results were negative. I was diagnosed with degenerative disc disease and arthritis in my right hip. However, there was no need for surgery. I could return to work at the end of the twelfth week. During all of that, I had to drive sixteen hours back home to Texas. My grandmother was ill and in her final days. God called her home on March 23, 2021. I made the 16-hour car ride back to South Dakota four days after she passed.

I had my final appointment scheduled at the Spine Center on March 30, 2021. But one thing remained, I was still in pain. I felt as if no one believed me. The doctor at the Spine Center said, "you are probably going to continue to have episodes. Just do your exercises at home. Well, the devil is a lie. I was not going to accept that. It's been more than two years. I have not had another episode. Praise be to God!

As soon as I returned from Texas, I had to return to work

full time with no restrictions. One thing remained. I was still in constant pain.

April 1, 2021, when I returned to work, I gave my manager a two-month notice. I did it out of courtesy because she had been so understanding of my situation. I wanted to give her an opportunity to find my replacement.

I remember saying to my mom, if every test is negative and there is no need for surgery, this must be spiritual. In March, the Lord started speaking to me about not returning to work. The Lord was also speaking to me through the book we read in our book club. The book talks about how reasoning leads to confusion. It also says reasoning occurs when a person tries to figure out the way behind something. Reasoning causes the mind to revolve around and around a situation, issue, or even tempting to understand all its intricate parts.

This chapter was pivotal to my healing. When I read this, I thought this is me!! It was like a ping pong ball going back and forth in my mind.

Matthew 16:8
O ye of little faith, why reason ye among yourselves?

I was an excessive planner. I constantly thought about one hundred different ways something could work or might work. I constantly said things like, if I do this, then I can do this. Or if I work until this date then I will get paid until this date. The reasoning made it difficult to make decisions or finish what I started. It caused me to be stuck. It caused me to be at that job longer than God wanted me to.

One night, in our mentorship group, the Pastor was talking about infirmities. At the time, I said, I do not have any infirmities. Truth be told, I did not really know what that word meant.

Infirmity - physical or mental weakness: disability, illness, sickness, ailment, disease, disorder, condition, indecision.

Disease, disorder, and indecision were the three words that described my situation. She referenced a book by Dr Henry W Wright, A More Excellent Way. I ordered the book that night. I began to search for his videos on YouTube. One of his videos he talks about degenerative disc disease. This was the diagnosis I was given. But I did not find out much from the video. The only thing I heard him say was "speak to the infirmity." I remember asking the Lord, "what is my infirmity?" "How do I speak to it?"

When I received the book, it said Degenerative Disc disease was tied to an addictive personality. I said to myself, I do not have an addictive personality because I have no addictions. Then I searched for the word sciatica. The book states, this disease is for which an evil spirit needs to be cast out. I said to myself, I do not have any evil spirits.

I had no clue what that even meant. I was still a baby in

Christ. I feel I always will be because as Christians we should always be learning. But here I was wondering, how could I have an evil spirit??

4 |

The Deliverance

My back pain became an excuse to sit and do nothing. I did nothing but sit on the couch, watch TV, and scroll through my phone. It is as if I was glued to the couch. It was as if the couch had a hold on me that would not let go. This went on for weeks. Even though my Chiropractor told me movement, walking was what I needed to do. I did not. I could not.

One night while I was scrolling through my phone, I "stumbled" upon a YouTube video where the young lady in the video talked about being delivered from laziness and procrastination. While I was watching her video, I could not believe what I was hearing. She was telling my story. I could not believe the similarities between our stories. She talked about a YouTube video she watched that helped her with deliverance from laziness and procrastination. I had no idea laziness and procrastination were attached to spirits.

God is so amazing!! That night he used a YouTube video to deliver a message to me. Remember in the last chapter I said Dr Wright's book mentioned for sciatica, evil spirits need to be cast out?? Well, here it was! The evil spirits I did not think I had were the spirits of laziness and procrastination. That night I asked God to deliver me from the spirit of procrastination, laziness, and slumber. All Glory to God!!

There was so much revelation that night. After that night, I began the process of taking part in my own healing. I learned God was waiting on me. I could no longer wait for him. He reminded me of the woman with the issue of blood. She sought after Jesus. She followed him until she touched the hem of his garment. The time had come for me to wholeheartedly chase after Jesus.

Luke 8:43-48

43 And a woman having an issue of blood twelve years, which had spent all her living upon physicians, neither could be healed of any, 44 Came behind him, and touched the border of his garment: and immediately her issue of blood stanched. 45 And Jesus said, who touched me? When all denied, Peter and they that were with him said, Master, the multitude throng thee and press thee, and sayest thou, who touched me? 46 And Jesus said, somebody hath touched me: for I perceive that virtue is gone out of me. 47 And when the woman saw that she was not hid, she came trembling, and falling down before him, she declared unto him before all the people for what cause she had touched him, and how she was

healed immediately. 48 And he said unto her, Daughter, be of good comfort: thy faith hath made thee whole; go in peace.

The Lord kept telling me to quit my job at the end of my two-month notice. But I did not listen. I extended my time by two weeks. I thought I was doing them a favor. I was being disobedient to God. They did everything they could to get me to stay.

I had a meeting with my manager on a Friday. She offered to allow me to work part time. She said I could work the hours I was able to work. She told me to think about it over the weekend. By this time, it was the first week of June. My notice was dated through the end of May.

During this entire process, I was declaring my trust in the Lord. I would say to the Lord, I trust you. It was time to show him. That Sunday at church, during worship, I said "Lord, I trust you". He said, "step through". I heard him loud and clear. He said, "if you trust me, step through".

On Monday, when I returned to work, my manager asked what I had decided. I said, I am done. A week later I was gone. My last day was June 16, 2021. And I never looked back. I had delayed my healing and deliverance by extending my time at work. I was disobedient to the Lord. I delayed the plan and purpose because I was trying to figure things out on my own.

In the process, I also learned reasoning was a control issue. I never finished what I started. I was always too busy reasoning with myself, trying to do things on my own. The Bible tells us in Matthew 6:33, Seek ye first the kingdom of God. At the time, I was not. I was trying to figure it out on my own. I was not asking God to lead and guide me. I did not ask for wisdom or clarity. Therefore, it was difficult for me to make decisions. I stayed at my job longer than I should have.

My back pain began to cause other issues. I had knee pain, neuropathy in my feet, and numbness in my right leg. I could not walk long distances or up the stairs. It felt like I was never going to get to the other side. But here I am. Praise God!! I am so grateful I am not where I was physically and spiritually. I had constant pain for a year and half.

The two years after I quit my job, I was able to focus on my healing and deliverance. Most importantly, this time allowed me to build my relationship with the Father, the Son, and the Holy Spirit. To go deeper in the things of God.

During that time, I had no idea God was creating a ministry in me and through me. When the Lord first told me, I would have a ministry. I could not believe it. I did not feel I was qualified. He reminded me that it is He who qualifies me.

I had to press in and allow God to be God. Now I can recognize the plots and schemes of the enemy. Now I know how to wield the weapons of spiritual warfare. Now I know

I have authority over the enemy. God has shown the power I have over the enemy. Now I know how to pray for myself and for others. Now I know the power and strength I have through the spirit of the Lord. Now I know why the enemy attacked my mind, body, and spirit.

God is no respecter of persons. If he can heal and deliver me. He can do the same for you. What was I trusting God to do? I trusted him to heal me, and I was trusting him financially. God is so good. He has never left me. Since I quit my job, God has provided week after week, month after month.

In the previous chapter I talked about my plan to work full time. But God had a different plan. Now that my daughter is in high school, I am still a stay-at-home mom. He told me to quit that job so He could birth a ministry in me and through me. I was able to spend more time with God.

God began to write my story, these stories that are written in the pages of this book and other books that will follow.

I had to break this curse so it would not affect generations to follow. In that season, the Lord began to teach me how to break generational curses. As for the writing of this book, do I know everything? NO! But I am constantly learning. Always a student of God's word.

What I learned in this season I want to impart to you in hopes it will help with your own deliverance.

● First, GIVE YOUR LIFE TO JESUS. The Bible says John 14:6

● Jesus answered, "I am the way, the truth, and the life. **No one comes to the Father except through me.**

● Recognize the curse (the stronghold). You must admit there is a problem. In the beginning I was in denial. I said to myself I do not have any evil spirits. The enemy played on that. If I did not recognize it, I couldn't confess it. Therefore, he would continue to have the upper hand. Now, I am no longer deceived. I can instantly recognize the attack and speak to it and against it with the word of God.

● Break the curse by applying God's word. Fight battles with spiritual weapons. **(Ephesians 6)**

● Align your words with God's word. Words can be evidence of your faith. Exchange negative words for positive words. **Proverbs 18:21** The tongue has the power of life and death, and those who love it will eat its fruit.

● Forgive people who hurt us. **Mark 11:25** And when you stand praying, if you hold anything against anyone, forgive them, so that your Father in heaven may forgive you your sins."

● Walk in obedience with God.

2 John 1:6 And this is love: that we walk in obedience to his commands. As you have heard from the beginning, his command is that you walk in love.

Set Apart

In 2007, while I was working for a large bank, I traveled to South Dakota for business. When I landed, I felt like I landed on Mars. I was a big city girl. Sioux Falls felt like a very small town. I was surprised they even had an airport.

Never in my dreams did I think I would live here. This town nor this state were never on my radar. When I was here for work, I never imagined I would live here. Before my daughter was born, I was interviewing for jobs in Arizona.

Matthew 19:29
And everyone who has left houses or brothers or sisters or father or mother or children or lands, for my name's sake, will receive a hundredfold and will inherit eternal life

One day, I was talking to my family, and I said, I still do

not know why I am here. I said it with an attitude. Like, "why am I still here, I should be gone by now!!"

For years, I did not like living here. South Dakota never felt like "home". Even after twelve years, it felt like a temporary place.

July 29, 2011, I moved from Texas to South Dakota. The move happened with such ease. Since then, I have been praying for a move back to Texas. My prayer has been that God would open a window of opportunity to move back. More specifically to the Dallas area. I never imagined I would live in South Dakota for twelve years.

Clearly God had other plans. One morning at the park, I said, Lord, why am I here?? When I made the move to South Dakota I did not consult you. But everything happened with such ease. Why was that?

I did not expect the Lord to answer so quickly. But God stopped me in my tracks when I heard him say, I did not move you here for your daughter's father or for your daughter. I moved you here for you. I moved you here to separate you from your past. I had to separate you from an ex-boyfriend, people, places, and things. I even had to separate you from your family. I had to set you apart so that you could be all I created you to be. Had you stayed you would have returned to the things of your past.

I do not think I ever heard him so clearly. I just stood there in the middle of the park, and I began to weep. At that moment, it all made sense to me. At that moment, I understood why I had to go through all of it. Looking back, had I stayed nothing in my life would have changed. I would have been more committed to the things of the world than building a relationship with my Lord and Savior.

Then the Lord reminded me of the story of Ruth. Like Ruth, I left my family, my friends, and my home to go to an unknown place. I could not imagine what would transpire. The Lord spoke to me and said, "you will never return to Moab." For me, my hometown represents Moab. A place where He said I could visit, but I would never go back there to live.

Everything I experienced in the last twelve years, the tests, the trials, the disappointments, the spiritual warfare. It all made sense! I understood why I had to go through all of it. During the last twelve years, I have developed a relationship with the Father, the Son, and the Holy Spirit. God has taken me through a process of growth. A refiner's fire is how I can describe it. Where I am becoming more spiritually mature, where he has stretched my faith.

1 Peter 1:6-9

In all of this you greatly rejoice, though now for a little while you may have had to suffer grief in all kinds of trials. These have come so that the proven genuineness of your faith refined by fire-may result in praise, glory, and honor when Jesus Christ is revealed. Though you have not seen him, you love him, and even though you do not see him now, you believe in him and are filled with an inexpressible and glorious joy, for you are receiving the end result of your faith, the salvation of your souls.

I realize now, there was something God wanted to do in me and through me. Now I know God had to set me apart to birth a ministry. That ministry began with one word from the Lord - Anchor. When I first heard that word, I had no idea what God meant. It took a couple of months for the Lord to reveal to me what Anchor meant. Until one day, the Lord said start a Podcast. I knew nothing about Podcasts. But I had to do what God told me to do.

One morning, when I pulled into my driveway, I heard God say, there is an ending here. At the time I did not know what that meant. I have always felt my time here in South Dakota is temporary. I know without a doubt, God is doing a new thing. In the meantime, I now know my assignment here is not complete.

I am so thankful for the insight God has given me about why I am in South Dakota. Before, I could not see past my complaints and frustrations. I did not want to live here for this long. I thought by now I would be living in Texas. But I must let God be God. I must trust that his plans are better than my own.

I learned everything God is doing in my life is not about me. It is because He has someone else in mind. When I learned that, I gained a whole new perspective.

I read a quote by Patrick Weaver Ministries that states: When God calls you to ministry, you will have trials that are not about you. They are for you to get the oil you need for the people God assigned to you.

Now my prayer is that God would enlarge my territory. I know he is going to change my address and geographical location. In the meantime, I will continue to do what He tells me to do.

It is BIGGER than me!!

6 |

Elevation Requires Separation

In 2022, the Lord removed two people from my life. "Friends" I had met shortly after moving to South Dakota. I was very close to these two ladies. Our children practically grew up together. We had a few things in common. We were from Texas or lived in Texas prior to moving to South Dakota. We took care of each other's children, we celebrated holidays and birthdays, and we traveled together. We were there for each other through the highs and the lows. These were seven- and ten-year friendships. We shared everything.

You may have heard the phrase, ELEVATION REQUIRES SEPARATION. I did not quite understand that statement when I first heard it. I am the type of person that wants the best for everyone. If something good happens to me, I want to share it with the people close to me. As I continued my walk with God, I realized not every friendship is going to be like the relationship of Naomi and Ruth. Where I go, you go. My God will be your God. Ruth 1:16 says, "Your God, will be my God." The more I started to build my relationship with God, I soon realized, my God was not their God.

The first person to leave my life, there were others before her, was the person I had a seven-year friendship with. September 2021, she asked if I would help plan her daughter's birthday party. This was not out of the ordinary for us, as we did this all the time. We decided to meet for coffee before we went shopping for party decorations. I asked her what the theme was for her daughter's party. She said the theme was Halloween and spooky.

It was no surprise to me because of her beliefs. She believed in New Age practices and doctrines. That day was the first time I had ever seen her wear a pentagram necklace. She also had a pentagram pop socket on her cell phone. She understood my beliefs. She said she even knew some of what was in the bible. However, she said she believed in a "higher power."

There is no "higher power" than God. I sat down in front of her and thought, this devil is not hiding anymore. By this time, I was beginning to question whether trick or treating or "celebrating" Halloween was for me and my family.

After the birthday party, I began to question our friendship. I would pray that one day she would be sitting next to me in church worshiping my God. I did not see her again until January 2022. She had informed me that she had been very ill for about two months. I continued to pray that she would come out from among them and build a relationship with the Lord and Savior Jesus Christ.

I was still questioning our friendship. But when I would talk to God about her, it is as if I was trying to justify the friendship. I would say "she's a good person". Or "she's not a bad person, she just believes differently." "But I pray one day she will change her heart for God". Then I heard the Lord say, "Stop praying for her" and give her no access. I had to cut all ties with her at that point. I had to remove and block her from social media. I also had to block her phone number. My obedience to God was more important than friendship.

Ephesians 5:11
And have no fellowship with the unfruitful works of darkness, but rather reprove them.

God places people in your life for a season. At the time, those friendships were necessary. Necessary for what I needed at the time. As I was drawing near to the Lord, he gave me a revelation about those friendships. He told me they cannot go where I am taking you.

The first-person God removed from my life was not just a friend, she was a coworker. When I left that job, I was able to get her a job at my new place of employment. Not once, but twice. I was trying to take her with me. I would have taken the second person with me too. But that was not the plan of the Lord.

The second person the Lord removed from my life was a friend I met shortly after I moved to South Dakota. It seemed as if we had a lot in common. We met through a Stay-at-Home Moms group. We were both from Texas. We became good friends very quickly. She was very kind and generous. We had fun together, we laughed together, and we experienced some heartbreak together. I considered her a good friend. We talked daily.

In case of emergencies, she knew she could call me. Even her children knew they could call on me. I did everything I could to support her. About eight years into the friendship, things began to shift. I was committed to attending church every Sunday and building a relationship with God.

Because she was going through a difficult time, I invited her to church. The morning she came, she was late. She had issues or "drama" that morning. After church we talked about the issue that prevented her from being on time. It seemed that the days were different, but the issues were the same. At the time I did not fully recognize what was happening to her.

As I began to grow spiritually, I was able to see her situation differently. A few months passed. Again, same issues on different days. I noticed there was no progress. She was in the same situation. I invited her to church again. She agreed to attend. Sunday came and went. She was a no show. Monday, I received a call from her with all the reasons she could not attend. She agreed to go the next Sunday. Again, Sunday came and went. She was a no show. Then came the excuses for not attending that Sunday. I concluded she was not ready.

As time passed, she revealed to me, "things" were happening in her home. I told her John 10:10 The thief comes only to steal and kill and destroy; I have come that they may have life and have it to the full. It was clear the enemy was attacking her from every angle.

One day, the Lord gave me a word for her. I said to her, "the enemy has come after your marriage, your health, your vehicles, and now your children." I asked her, "what more is it going to take? What more are you going to allow the enemy to take from you before you have enough?" I felt the enemy had also robbed her of her peace.

One day I told her I felt as if some friendships needed to end. More specifically the first-person God removed. She knew about the first friend that God removed because she was an unbeliever. She knew about the dark things she was involved in. Then she asked if I was referring to our friendship. I was honest and told her I had questioned it.

By this time, I felt the friendship had become one sided. It was all about the drama in her life. The hours on the telephone discussing the drama had become draining. I was going through things on my own. My guess is, she assumed all was perfect in my life because she never asked, Sandra, how are YOU doing? How are things in Sandra's world? I feel like she could not see past everything going on in her life.

The doors had to close on these friendships so God could make way for divine connections and relationships. Connections that would help advance his Kingdom.

The hours on the phone were a distraction to keep me from spending time with the Lord. It was a pause in the process to the purpose. Once those doors closed, things became clearer. I had clarity. I was able to press in. I was able to spend time with Jesus. I was able to grow in my walk with God.

I pray for them, I want the best for them, and I hope one day they choose to follow Jesus. The Lord used me to plant the seed. My prayer is that God would send the laborers to water the seeds.

If they were ever to reach out to me for prayer, I would gladly do it. But only under the direction and guidance of the Lord.

7 |

7 The Dark Cloud

One night, I had a dream about me and my daughter. We were walking down the street. Behind us, I noticed a dark cloud coming towards us. I said to my daughter, let's step into this hotel until the storm passes. We walked into the hotel lobby. I said to my daughter, "you wait in the lobby away from the window. I'm going to look out until it passes." As I'm standing at the window looking out, there's a person standing to the left and right of me. I had no idea who they were.

As I'm looking out of the window, in the sky, there forms a dragon and a heart with two daggers in it. But it never rained. I woke up out of my sleep and asked the Lord, "what was that about?"

"What was the meaning of this dream? "The next morning the Lord led me to:

Revelation 12:17 KJV
And the dragon was wroth with the woman and went to make war with the remnant of her seed, which keep the commandments of God, and have the testimony of Jesus Christ.

After I read that, I thought, this enemy is mad at me. This helped me to understand the reason my daughter was in the dream. Then I asked the Lord, "why is this enemy angry with me?"

The Lord said two things to me:
Remember the birthday party you helped plan? She said her daughter loved dragons.

The enemy is angry with you because you've been praying for her. My prayer for her was that one day she would be standing next to me in church worshiping my God.

At the time, her daughter was only ten years old. I learned through Revelation 12:17, dragons represent the enemy.

That explained the dragon. But what about the dark cloud and the heart with two daggers. Most likely if you Google the heart with two daggers you get the new age, tarot card interpretation. Since that is not of God, I waited for Him to reveal it.

One morning during our mentorship call, our Pastor began to speak about a black cloud. She said the black cloud stood for a curse. This was confirmation of the black cloud in my dream. My interpretation was that the spirit she carried was trying to curse me and my daughter. In my dream, the hotel was my shelter. This dream was a warning. Thankfully in this season of my life I was learning to pray against those spirits. During that time Psalm 91 was the scripture I had been reading daily.

The Lord is my fortress.

Psalm 91:1-16

He that dwelleth in the secret place of the Most High Shall abide under the shadow of the Almighty. I will say of the LORD, He is my refuge and my fortress: My God; in him will I trust. Surely, he shall deliver thee from the snare of the fowler, And from the noisome pestilence. He shall cover thee with his feathers, and under his wings shalt thou trust: His truth shall be thy shield and buckler. Thou shalt not be afraid for the terror by night; Nor for the arrow that flieth by day; Nor for the pestilence that walketh in darkness; Nor for the destruction that wasteth at noonday. A thousand shall fall at thy side, and ten thousand at thy right hand; But it shall not come nigh thee. Only with thine eyes shalt thou behold and see the reward of the wicked. Because thou hast made the LORD, which is my refuge, Even the most High, thy habitation; There shall no evil befall thee, neither shall any plague come nigh thy dwelling. For he shall give his angels charge over thee, to keep thee in all thy ways. They shall bear thee up in their hands, lest thou dash thy foot against a stone. Thou shalt tread upon the lion and adder:

The young lion and the dragon shalt thou trample under
feet. Because he hath set his love upon me, therefore will I
deliver him: I will set him on high, because he hath known
my name. He shall call upon me, and I will answer him: I will
be with him in trouble; I will deliver him and honor him.
With long life will I satisfy him,
And shew him my salvation.

It took a while for God to reveal the meaning of the heart
with the two daggers through it. In this situation some people
might have referenced other doctrines to try to find the meaning. But I knew, if God showed it to me in a dream, He would
have an explanation for it. Eventually the Lord led me to this
scripture.

Psalm 37:14-15
The wicked have drawn out the sword, and have bent
their bow, to cast down the poor and needy, and to slay such
as be of upright conversation
Their swords shall enter their own heart, and their bows
shall be broken.

Afterwards the Lord revealed to me the dark cloud was a
curse trying to come upon me and my daughter. I understood
the reason God told me to stop praying for her. She wasn't
willing to change. This was the final confirmation of what
He had spoken to me about her. This time He allowed me
to see it through a Facebook post. She had posted a photo of
an alcoholic beverage with a skull on the label. In the photo,

there looked to be a candle, and a jar with sand and twigs. What was most alarming was a book she had that said the word demonology in the title. Her post said something like, having a drink and conjuring spirits. I knew at that point, there was no turning back.

It saddened me because I could literally see changes in her countenance. The dark eyes, the skin condition. I could sense sadness. Not because she told me she suffered from depression. It was as if she was being tormented in her mind. She did her best to look happy, but I could tell she wasn't. She struggled financially and she accepted that as her lot in life. She believed the lies of the enemy.

I planted the seeds of God's word throughout our friendship. However, my hope for her is that laborers would water those seeds.

8

Speak My Word

Everything God is doing in my life is not just for me, it's because He has someone else in mind. Praise God.

When God began to tell me to Speak His Word, I had a dream. In my dream when I opened my eyes, I was sitting face to face with the enemy. He had his hands out as if he wanted me to place my hand in his.

In my dream I was trying to speak, my mouth was moving, but there was no sound coming out of my mouth. I kept trying to say the name Jesus. With each attempt, the name of Jesus began to come from my mouth. I kept saying Jesus, Jesus, Jesus. When I began to scream the name of Jesus, the enemy disappeared.

Philippians 2:9-11 KJV
Wherefore God also hath highly exalted him and given

him a name which is above every name: that at the name of Jesus every knee should bow, of things in heaven, and things in earth, and things under the earth; and that every tongue should confess that Jesus Christ is Lord, to the glory of God the Father.

When I woke up from that dream, I said to the Lord what was going on? It wasn't until a few weeks later the Lord revealed to me that the enemy was trying to silence me. He was trying to mute me.

Philippians 3:14 KJV

I press toward the mark for the prize of the high calling of God in Christ Jesus

April 2022, this was my statement: "Lord, I give you permission to use me. I accept the assignment. Yes, you can use me for your purpose. Release the purpose and plans." Be careful what you say to the Lord. Be mindful. I say that so you can prepare yourself for what's to come. I had no idea what was about to happen in my life.

Then I began to hear the Lord say, "SPEAK MY WORD." I said, okay Lord. Then I began to ask the Lord a million and one questions. To whom, when, where, how??

The Lord went silent on me and didn't confirm my questions. But every now and then, I would hear him say "SPEAK MY WORD." Then the confirmations began.

May 12, 2022, my Pastor, and Mentor spoke these words. (prophesied) This was a word from the Lord: There are souls that are lost, and no one is giving them the right direction. Some of my children are afraid to lead them in the right way. Be my witness, be the extended hand of Me, share my word, share your story. Tell them who I am. Draw them back to me through my Holy Spirit. Tell them I hear them and see them.

The very next day, I woke up praising and worshiping the Lord. I felt the power of the Holy Spirit come upon me. Later that morning, I got in my car, still worshiping the Lord, weeping, driving to the local coffee shop and back; then the Lord dropped this phrase in my spirit; I KNEW HER WHEN. He said, when people from your past see where I am taking you, people that have been removed from your life they will say I KNEW HER WHEN.

It's as if the Lord was allowing me to hear what they would say. I heard things like, well I knew her when she was out at the club. Yes, we used to party together. How can God use her?? Or they would say, yes, I know her. We used to hang out all the time. We were good friends. Or they will say, yes, I know her, that's family. The Lord said to me, they will try to attach themselves to you in this season.

Not everyone is an assignment. Some people are like attachments. Unfortunately, I've had the ones sent as attachments. Those who were attachments, God used as a lesson in discernment. Now I'm equipped to recognize them quickly instead of investing time to try to figure them out.

During this time, the Lord taught me those sent as attachments will at times want to "borrow" your faith. This prevents them from building their own relationship with God. They see the favor of God in your life, so they try to connect or reconnect. Beware of the attachments. Some people are in your life for a season. Be not deceived by seasonal people.

In all of this, the Lord said to me, your stories give me glory. So here we go!

May 25, 2022, I heard God say GREEN LIGHT, GO!!

May 31, 2022, My Pastor, and Mentor said these words from the Lord(prophesied):
"Go! Tell them I am here! Go! Tell them the enemy's plans against their life cannot succeed. Go! Tell them I love them. Tell them I am here for them. Tell them your story! Be my witness!"
I knew then this was my confirmation. The very next day I made the decision to partner with God and start a Podcast. The Podcast - I Knew Her When. I knew nothing about Podcasts. But God kept confirming this was a way to speak his word.

1 Corinthians 3:9
For we are labourers together with God.

June 1, 2022, My Pastor, and Mentor said these words from the Lord(prophesied) "I chose this time to call you to be my witness. For this time is crucial. Yet fragile, delicate, nothing to play with. I chose this time to remind you to share my word, share my love and to be My people. Share who I am, share me with the ones who are lost, who have yet to find me."

Psalm 62:11-12
God hath spoken once, twice have I heard this; That power belongeth unto God. Also, unto thee O Lord Belongeth mercy; For thou renderest to every man according to his work.

June 24, 2022, I received the next confirmation. Our Pastor spoke these words from the Lord: "Go! Go speak My word. Know my truth. Stand in your faith. For I am standing with you. That morning before I heard our Pastor speak those words, the Lord led me to Isaiah 12:4 - And on that day you will say, give thanks to the Lord, call on his name, Make His deeds known among the peoples; Proclaim that His name is exalted.

During this time the Lord was telling me to speak his word, He told me to speak it on a Podcast. Not YouTube. Not Facebook live. Not Instagram. I knew nothing about

Podcasts. But the Lord gave me knowledge and understanding to begin with.

July 6, God confirmed His word again!! This time He said through our Pastor, "Speak my word. For you are waiting for me to move. I am waiting for you to speak my word. Speak My word moves heaven." Then the Lord said, "I am speaking into your life this day. Speak My words, says the Lord. Believe my word. Speak My words, speak my truth. Be consistent in speaking my word. Be consistent. Consistency builds a house. But my word builds nations. Speak My word. Believe in me. Have faith in me. Have faith in my word. Have faith in me.

I received confirmation after confirmation during this process. I share the timeline with you to show you how strategic God is.

9

A Man Named Ricky

July 13, 2022, while we were in Texas, we had plans to meet my cousin and her husband for lunch. We arrived at the restaurant early. As my daughter and I were walking into the restaurant, we walked past a gentleman sitting on the ground. As we were walking past, he looked at me and said, "God bless you". I said "likewise".

After we were seated at our table, I began to shake my head. The power of the Holy Spirit fell upon me at that moment. I couldn't stop shaking my head. My daughter asked, "Mom, are you ok?" It was like I could hear her in the distance but at the same time I was asking the Lord, " what is going on?" "What is happening?"

I began to feel a sense of urgency. I asked our server, "What do you know about the man outside?" "I don't want to get him in any trouble, but what can you tell me about him?" She said, "we have found him sleeping in our game room."

We placed our order and I said to her, "I need a cheeseburger, fries and a cup of water to go. Can you bring it out with our order?" She said, "yes".

After a few minutes, I excused myself from the table and walked to the restroom. I was still feeling this sense of urgency. I couldn't shake it. I walk back to our table. Our server was bringing our food out. I didn't see the order. I said to her, " I don't want to be rude, but where is my order to go? I need it as soon as you can bring it out." She went back to the kitchen. A couple of minutes later she brought out the to-go order and water.

I excused myself from the table again. I took the food and water. I walked outside to search for the gentleman sitting on the ground. I walked up to him and asked, "what is your name?" He said, "My name is Ricky." I said, "Ricky, do you believe in the Lord?" He said, "Yes, ma'am, I do." I said, "Ricky, the Lord told me to buy you lunch today."

I handed him his lunch, I placed my hand on his shoulder, he took his cap off, and I began to pray for him. I don't remember much about what came out of my mouth when I prayed for him. I do know I prayed Numbers 6:24-26 over him, I prayed for healing in his body and the renewing of his mind.

I thanked him for allowing me to buy his lunch. I walked back into the restaurant and sat still for a moment. I couldn't come out of the realm that I was in. My family asked what happened. I told them without too many details.

A week later, I returned to South Dakota. Amid being on vacation back home in Texas, I missed most of the lives from our mentorship group the week before. When I returned to South Dakota, I settled in and watched the replay of all the lives.

During the live broadcast for July 13, 2022, our Pastor spoke about a vision of someone shaking their head. She demonstrated the shaking of the head. She said, "their head was just shaking going back and forth. And there was darkness surrounding them. The spirit of confusion was upon them. This person was shaking, moving, twisting, turning. That is the enemy trying to take their mind." She said she was sad because it wasn't a good sight to see.

I paused the video, called my daughter over, (she's 12 years old at the time.), I said, "watch this". I played it back for her. She said, "mom, that's what you were doing at the restaurant. She said, "How does Pastor know your life?" I said, "she doesn't! That's the Holy Spirit." I asked my daughter what day we were at the restaurant. My daughter said, Wednesday. I looked back on my calendar to find out what day I met Ricky. July 13 was on Wednesday, the day I met him.

Through this encounter he was not only using me to minister to Ricky, but he was also teaching me. The very next day, the Lord spoke to me and said, "she's watching you in your ministry." He was talking about my daughter.

I honestly feel like Ricky was sent to that very place by God. This was the first opportunity the Lord had given me to "speak His word" like He had instructed me to. This was the first act of obedience to the Lord in real time. That's the only way I can describe it. God spoke and I had to answer the call immediately. I feel like Ricky was my test of obedience, to see if I would do what the Lord instructed me to do.

Psalm 41:1
Blessed is he that considereth the poor;
The Lord will deliver him in time of trouble

10 ▎

The Instruction

February 2022, I bowed low before the Lord face down, weeping, surrendering all. I said Lord, I give you permission to use me. I accept the assignment. You can use me for the purpose and the plans. That was my statement to God.

Two months later, April 2022, the Lord said, Speak My Word. I said OK Lord. To whom? When? Where? The Lord went silent on me. But occasionally God would say Speak My Word. One day he said to me Ezekiel 2:7. I looked it up and it says:

Ezekiel 2:7

Speak My Word whether they listen or not for they are a rebellious people.

That scripture was my confirmation.

June 2022 the Lord told me to start a Podcast. I knew

nothing about Podcasts. With the help of the Holy Spirit leading and guiding me, I started a Podcast called I KNEW HER WHEN. I recorded a few episodes and thought, this is it. This is how God wants me to speak his word. It was a way to speak His word. But this would not be the only way.

July 2022 God presented me with the first opportunity aside from the Podcast to speak his word to a man named Ricky sitting outside of a restaurant. From there the Lord began to place me in situations where I had to speak his word.

September 30, 2022, I attended a Women's Conference in Atlanta, GA. I was seated at the second table from the back. I heard the presenter announce my name as a recipient of the When Sisters Unite Sister of the Year Award. I sat at the table for a moment, thinking, did I just hear my name called? I stood up and thought, am I supposed to walk to the stage?

As I was walking to the stage from the back of the room, I remember feeling as if I was walking alone. I didn't see any-one to the left or the right of me. It was as if the Lord was walking me through the secret place to get to the stage. When I stepped on the stage I said, thank you Jesus. I walked back to my seat in awe of what the Lord had done for me. Receiving that honor had nothing to do with me. But God!! It was by his spirit that I received that award.

October 2, 2022, at Center of Hope Church, the Lord spoke to me and said, "You will carry the mantle for your family." I sat in the pew, and I began to weep. And again, I bowed low before the Lord and said yes. Be mindful of what you say to God, He will take you at your word. After the conference, I wrote a note to myself that said, Next year, I will return to this conference as______. I filled in the blank with only one word.

April 2023, a year after I bowed low before God, I received a call I never expected. I received a call informing me that I was the last speaker selected for the When Sisters Unite Conference in October 2023. The organizer of the conference asked me to take a few days, pray about it. In 2022, it was prophesied that I would be speaking to a large group of women. I received confirmation a few days before I received the call.

The Bible says: Joshua 1:3 - I will give you every place where you set your foot, as I promised Moses
Deuteronomy 11:24 says Every place where you set your foot will be yours
Immediately, I said yes! In June, the Lord began to show me what he wanted me to speak about. He began to demonstrate his power to me in numbers and number of days.

Let's not confuse this with new age practices, numerology, or angel numbers. That is not biblical or from God.
There are numbers in the bible that have meaning. For example:
Three is the number of completion
Five is the number of grace

Seven is the number of perfection

Eight is the number of new beginnings

The number two in the Bible represents a union, or unity between Christ and His church, or between a husband and wife.

Ecclesiastes 4:9-10 Two are better than one, for if either of them falls, one can help the other up.

Matthew 18:16 But if he will not hear thee, then take with thee one or two more, that in the mouth of two or three witnesses every word may be established.

Matthew 18:19-20 that if two of you shall agree on earth as touching anything that they shall ask, it shall be done for them of my Father which is in heaven.

As I mentioned earlier, I wrote a note to myself after the 2022 conference saying I would return to the conference as one word. But God had other plans. God took the pen from my hand, drew a line across that word, and said NO! The Lord said, "what you have written would keep you hidden and anonymous."

The Lord said you will return to the conference as a Speaker, a Sister of the Year Nominee, you will return with a Kingdom business, you will return as an author, you will return mantled like Esther to reach back for your family, to reach back for my people. I will anoint you like Jael, to drive a stake through the temple of the enemy.

I have sent you back to take your position and speak my

word whether they listen to you or not. This wasn't a question from the Lord. It was a command from our General, a command from Jehovah Sabaoth, the host of armies.

I challenge you to write a note to yourself that says, next year I will be _______. And for three hundred and sixty-five days, fifty-two weeks, twelve months, one day at a time hand over the pen and allow the Lord to fill in the blank. In Jesus name!!

The Bible says to whom much is given much is required. When God gives you an instruction to accept the responsibility and take your position, He's calling you higher.

After the conference things begin to shift. The conference activated me, and I began to experience the deeper things of God. In this season, after the conference, he taught me about the position of a Watchman.

Ezekiel 3:16-17

At the end of seven days the word of the Lord came to me: "Son of man, I have made you a watchman for the people of Israel; so, hear the word I speak and give them warning from me.

The Lord started to wake me up at all hours of the night. At first, I thought, I'll just get up, go to the bathroom, go back to sleep. That wasn't it. The Lord began to speak to me through dreams. In the middle of the night God would give me instructions and have me intercede in prayer for his people.

Once I realized what the Lord was doing, I would wake up, ask God, what are my instructions? He would give me one word and teach me what it meant. He would download a word in the Spirit for his people. He would have me pray against wickedness in high places during third watch.

I remember there was a period of two weeks, where God was calling me almost every night. I would wake up and ask what are my instructions, Lord? For two weeks I barely slept. But God!! He gave me rest. He also gave me the strength to get through the day when I had but a couple of hours of sleep.

Exodus 33:14

And He said, "My presence shall go with you, and I will give you rest."

What I understand now, is everything I went through in this season was preparation. A season of learning. A season of growth by the Spirit of God. A season where the oil was produced. A season of impartation. A season where He taught me about the full armor of God. So, I could war in the spirit for His people. A season where God made me a watchman for his people. A season where He taught me about the weapons of warfare; praise and worship, fasting and praying. A season that made me Battle Ready, to war in the Spirit, for His people! All Glory and Honor to God.

Hallelujah!

Acknowledgement

First and foremost, all Glory and Honor to God, who brought me out of darkness into his marvelous light. This journey with the Father, the Son, and the Holy Spirit has been an indescribable but awe-inspiring experience. This journey was so unexpected but so beautiful.

Those who dwell in the secret place of the Most High. That was my dwelling place. If I could put it into words, this is how I could describe it, under his wings. God was and is my refuge, my safe place. I never imagined this is where I would be when the Lord began a good work in my life. I have been stretched in ways I never imagined. He has taken me to new heights. I had no idea, the gifts and purpose that lay dormant in my life. Until I surrendered all to the Lord.

This was about discovering who God created me to be. My identity in Christ. It is no longer I, but he who lives in me. The life which I now live in the flesh I live by the faith of the Son of God, who loved me, and gave himself for me.

Words cannot express my gratitude for my best friend, Yolanda Myers. Your obedience to the Lord to prophesy, pray, encourage, and cover. What God put together forty years ago, cannot be broken. Yolanda, thank you for loving and covering my family. I am so grateful for our sisterhood and friendship.

To my Pit Crew, my divine connections, my sisters in Christ: Amy Bearden, Shywonna Brown, Latonia Barbour, Karen Brown-Frisby, I am so thankful to have you in my life. I love our sisterhood. God was so strategic the way he brought us together. From our first When Sisters Unite Conference in Atlanta, GA in 2022, to today, I cherish our conversations, and our travels.

What I love the most is how we are all in one accord. God is so amazing! We are forever bonded by the miracle the Lord allowed us to witness. The miracle of the Lord restoring the sight of our sister Shywonna. Our new normal will now be miracles, signs, and wonders.

Pastor JJ Fox-Hatch, my pastor, and my covering. I thank you for your love and encouragement. I never imagined I would be where I am today. But here I am living in the purpose and the plan God has for me. Thank you for acknowledging me when I stumbled upon your Facebook live. That was no accident. God knew what I needed when I found you. That day I found my Elijah.

It is an honor to be in close proximity to you Woman of God. I want to thank you for covering me and my family. Thank you for loving us the way you do. Thank you for encouraging us to go after everything God has for us. Thank you for your discipleship.

Most importantly to my family, Doug, and Olivia, thank

you for your love and support during this process. When I began my walk with God, I never imagined my walk would lead me to publish a book the Lord has written about my life over the last few years. It has been a journey.

Thank you for the times I had to be away from home to fulfill the call of God in my life. I am forever grateful for your love and support. To God be the glory for the things he has done and will continue to do for each of us.

What God put together cannot be separated.

About the Author

Sandra Carrizales was born and raised in Lubbock, Tx. She is a graduate of Wayland Baptist University.

Sandra is the founder of Speak My Words Ministries. Speak My Words Ministries is a teaching, intercessory, fasting and praying ministry. Her ministry is rooted in the foundation of Ezekiel 2:7. Sandra is also the founder and co-host of THE PANEL, a bible based, Christ centered Podcast.

Sandra is a 2022, 2023 and 2024 When Sisters Unite Sister of the Year Nominee. In 2022, Sandra was a recipient of the When Sisters Unite Sister of the Year award. In 2023 and 2024, she had the honor and privilege to return to When Sisters Unite Conference as a Conference Speaker.

www.ingramcontent.com/pod-product-compliance
Lightning Source LLC
Chambersburg PA
CBHW031413160726
47993CB00003B/1216